The Gutter Spread Guide to Prayer

AUTUMN
HOUSE PRESS

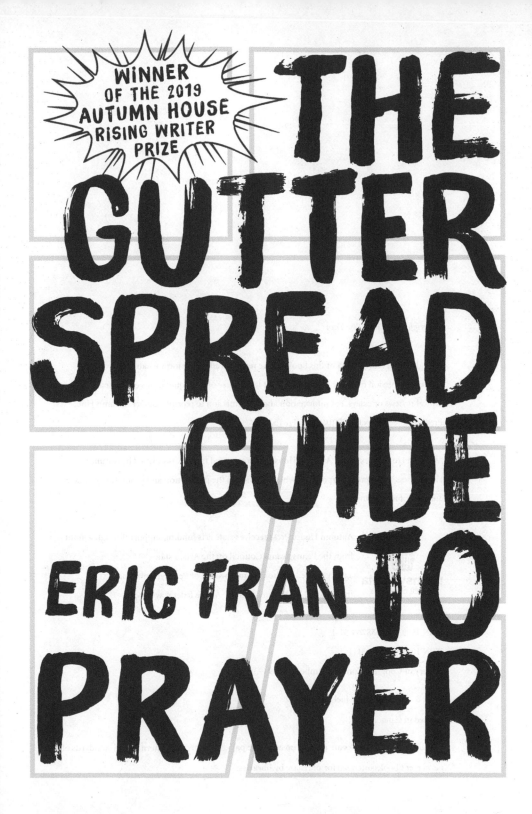

WINNER OF THE 2019 AUTUMN HOUSE RISING WRITER PRIZE

THE GUTTER SPREAD GUIDE TO

ERIC TRAN

PRAYER

Autumn House Press receives state arts funding support through a grant from the Pennsylvania Council on the Arts, a state agency funded by the Commonwealth of Pennsylvania, and the National Endowment for the Arts, a federal agency.

ISBN 13: 978-1-938769-51-1

ISBN 10: 1-938769-51-1

Library of Congress Control Number: 2019949362

Book & cover design by Joel W. Coggins

Printed in Canada

All Autumn House books are printed on acid-free paper and meet the international standards of permanent books intended for purchase by libraries.

for Zach

CONTENTS

III

Starting with a Line by Joyce Byers

Stranger Things S1, E1

You're talking about grief.
    This is different,
how the sky lost
    a single stitch and paid
the earth a debt
    of silver, a fortune
in nickels bruising
    the summer fruit.
Today the trains
    collapsed into prayer,
the river spat up
    its mudbed
like a fevered child.
    Witness the shapeless
effigy. The stars
    knocked loose
from god's mouth,
    cities drained
dead of color, futile
    in stop-and-go
monotone. I'm saying
    the dogwoods
cried themselves
    sterile and still
my friend is gone.

Recommendation

The clerk at Ultimate Comics says
If you didn't think you needed
Lois Lane and Catwoman drunk at brunch

and dear god do I have need
of the Midnighter who, between the gutters,
laughs because his lover left him

—what joy to feel again. I need
a giant alien bulldog hunting
his lost, mute master across hells.

The former sorcerer supreme losing
his love of magic and being rescued
by an ancient tree. Time-traveling

teens who visit their future
selves: happy. Who'd have thought?
Give me *kapow*! Give me *shazam*! Give

a one shot with perfect speech bubbles
where people know exactly what they want
to say. Give me a fantasy hour

where my friend is alive. A life of color
ink bleeding on my fingers.
Paper is paper is some days all

I feel I have. Give me the omnibus, the omniverse
with the immortal beings. Prove the world's
still held intact by its staples

Lectio Divina: Emma Frost

New X-Men #122

To her mutant students:
"The whole world is watching
us now. We must be nothing
less than fabulous."

. . .

My precious rejects who wake
to apocalypse. What do we lose
in fire? We are born
from flame, the treasure
man stole from gods.

. . .

Your creation thought
his skin too scarred
for me, but for him
I carried a bag of stones
to the river and witnessed
his wrist flick their weight
across the water.

. . .

The sun bears a gaze too
and has no response.
Praise, it feeds and blinds,
warms without so much
as a single word.

Pulse

Us and blindfold
in delicious dark. Done deaf

by bassline, scouting heat
with bladed tongues. Breath

a scream spun in reverse
and Lord we holler

wet down each other's
necks. Rapture and rupture,

every sizzled bead
of black sweat

spit swollen out
our skin. O god

make naked a flaw
with climax steeping

our glotted throats.
Give name the hollow

wont to fill fat
with blood. Sing us

a lie: our hearts
fed thick with thrust

and rhythm, sacred
fist made habit

the gasp and surrender
of living this soft.

Days after Orlando I Read the X-Men

who also tried paradise once. Genosha, a mutant slave island they freed
and claimed back. But even then, safety—that sugar-glass promise of
dancing chainless—centered them for retribution. Issue #115, after wild
sentinels with deadened eyes, after smoke and rubble, one mutant there
still breathed—she turned herself hard as diamond. Giant-sized issue #1,

another island: the team followed a distress call, but the mutant
was the fist of earth itself. Vines and fault lines trying to crumble
buildings. Imagine: all those homes atop that grieving face. But really,
any episode they practiced wearing such dusk: #25, Iceman sculpts a
doppelgänger and watches a brainwashed ally shatter that frozen dummy

formless; the friend-foe mourns so much he finally remembers his
humanity. #38, Jean Grey holds her dying demon clone, who, faced
with a legacy of second-tier loved one, kamikazes their psychic link.
Last panel, she's spread supine like a bludgeoned raven. #24, Kitty Pryde
phases a cosmic bullet right through Earth but can't release the death

she's stopped. I know, metaphors painted so thick the layers won't dry,
but this all feels like web and tissue. I mean I'm still staring right into
the blaring eclipse of also wanting that ungloved touch, my blue fur
unmatted and combed out clean. No mutation can stop such burning.
Maybe I teleport but only via a hell dimension. Shape-shift, more wolf

and fanged than I can bear. Early on the Professor made ruby-quartz
glasses to soothe the eyes' work—but even then the world tints redder still.

A Favor

I'm learning a favor
can be wrapped like a gift
     if someone wants to feel
     needed and there's so much
I want to tell him
I'm tired but not in a sad sense
     but like when he stayed up
     looking at Adam Rippon
in a harness (*twink nonsense* he'd say)
or deftly coded messages
     like me not skipping leg day.
     and saying *I'm doing butt stuff*
or when I forgot the word for rain
in Spanish and settled for *the sky*
     is crying and since we're talking
     about it I'd tell him I'm sad
just sad because with him
it was OK to sit in a storm
     of sad without unpacking
     the galoshes or an almanac
and this week I'm graduating
from medical school and wow
     so suddenly all the people I'll save
     who aren't him and right in the eye
of this I cracked my first joke
right clean like a tooth it's so nice
to tell someone I can still laugh
     without him and with him at once
     god I'm laughing so hard
my eyes are watering—look!
My whole shirtfront is drenched

Portrait in Pleather Tee

with fire doors propped open with freight
lift fraught

with mirrors with club choked with drag
queens making cheap

Asian driver jokes making
cheap *sorrys* with rail pours of two fingers

we left on the bar
with answering the door

for men looking just
how they said they did

years ago with refuge
under sheets with rebuffed

foot traffic with horn and roar
of leaving silenced

with suitcase packed in short
sleeves with sun chased

by cereal milk with long straw
breathing

with baking soda and bathtub with busted
pot sputtering black

brewed by the spoonful with smiling
daddies at happy hour

with town guides because of your cute
friends with tour of docks

after dark with midnight of bodies
pressed into bodies

with filling every cavity of dune
face with nervous giggling at the grunt

of human want with pause with voice
and breath enough

to scold *quit laughing you're
down here too*

Eloisa—

how to explain the bathhouse to you, how I buy pricey eucalyptus soap
because that's what dissolves in the steam-room mist. I don't like the
smell—I think it's rich fool's mint, but once a yoga instructor dotted
eucalyptus oil on my temples, and I was taken back to that steam room,
to the shadows of bodies against mist. I thought of how to describe the
appeal of anonymity of both subject and object and I stupidly thought
of party mix, where no single item tastes good really, but in the context
each handful feels right on your tongue. Last night, the men stood like
ancient statues until one of them wandered into the corner. Without any
signal, other men followed one by one, made a mass of limbs and grunts.
Eloisa, I wonder if what I mean to tell you is wandering the hallways of
by-the-hour rooms—waiting to catch any lingering glance—is like some
sex-starved Orpheus or Theseus chasing his bull-hung minotaur. That I
found him, my lover ghost or half-beast, in the heart of the maze, sitting
in the mist like a grand mountain, that he was the only man I touched
that night, that he came in my mouth without warning or a move to
return the gesture. Maybe what I mean to tell you is leaving the maze,
minimally scathed but also prizeless, skin still hungry for warmth, and
stopping by the water fountain to rinse or swallow. The man walked
by me, that he was still somehow a dark sylph I can't describe, that he
reached out to grab my wrist and gave it a gentle squeeze goodbye.

Explaining Again Why I Can't Give Blood

I'm told my veins are plump with death.
Since the day I licked salt and rust

from another boy's lips, my life
bled risk and want of risk, and

maybe that's how I want it:
to be alive, to swell

with song for my lovers'
lovers. Because we are blood

meals for the flower beds.
The pseudo-lillies, not

the perennials no one wants
to take a knife to. I've no blood

to give because someone's claimed it
for their own hands. I'm told

I am full of danger
but I'm only what's been fed to me.

My Mother Asks How I Was Gay
before Sleeping with a Man

She says I've taught you this before: press the skin
of pears to your nose to sense if they're ripe.
Sound out foreign words, spring-load them on your lips

before flicking them off your tongue. Measure drinks
with your fingers, test gold with your teeth. Do you trust
the strength of ice with the weight of one toe,

the day's weather without throwing yourself into it,
the spice of a pepper by biting the tip? Son,
the world is not known by its surfaces alone.

When you cut new flowers, split their stems
like a giant vein, teach them to drink water again.
I warned you once not to touch fire-red coils,

but you had to reach out your hand, palm the heat,
hold the fire in your fist to learn how to be afraid.

Compromise

I know I'm not alone
when I dream of him
    or wonder *what if*
because when news breaks
    in winter my aunts ask
if I knew him if
    he was gay the first winter
they've said *gay*
    so gently though not
suicide at least at first
    or remark how similar
his reflection was to mine
    gay and/or *depressed* and/or *Asian*
we know silence
    or I should say fear
nursed fat by love
    draws a circle around us
builds us a home
    in the rain and there
over a pot of new rice
    warm and plumped
like a fresh garden bed
    I don't ask if they dream
what will become of me
    when I'll reveal myself
as a dark endless cave
    under collapse I don't
dream I reassure them
    but I see him crying
singing as cranes do
    and I leap from bed
my arms flecked
    with feathers and I chase
him under
    a moon we don't
think to admire

I Tell My Mother about My Depression

She is ashamed of my seasickness,
her son, bled down from boat people.

We are kidding, of course. Between waves
and prayers to Mercy, she swore

her child would never know
the damp of hunger in his bones.

She wanted him fat like clay
and just as soft. In college, I lost

ten pounds of myself and half
the words she sang to me as a baby.

The aunties cooed my new frame
but she was silent, both of us famished

for the words we meant. I say
I'm sad from sun to sun

and her response is a crisp
twenty for the quiet burger joint

we visited when I was young
and never talked, or didn't need

words, our mouths and bellies
singing the same full rhythm.

Ode to My Morning Meds

Tossed to my
mouth's silk
night sky
where live
the lion
and lovers
and the archer
whose lyre
begged
a muse
to make
of thunder
applause
some great
weeping
of joy
beat like
boughs
in a storm
picking
off petals
like scabs
open buds
where fruit
will bloom

Your Doppelgänger

I go to his gym and eye-
fuck him without mercy.
      Jokes, jokes: grief

is blind to mercy,
a bat to the dark it splits
      right through.

He's most gorgeous
in periphery, transient rainbow
      in sprinkler water.

My god, the metaphors
I wrench in place to convince me
      he isn't you.
      I swear

every crack is a door
if you lean in hard. Every second
      a second chance. The paper-

width of light between a moment
of silence and a moment
      with silence. In one we

mourn. In another, I almost
whisper to him *please*
         don't jump

Lectio Divina: Hektor the Assassin

Saga #9

"Ooh, you gonna kill
us all with your faggy
laser sword?"

• • •

Dazzling glitter
stick, overwintered lily
swish. Flaming red wet
dream: here's my heart,
       my softest parts.

• • •

I wish men
who called me
faggot in a truck
whizzing by or with fists
bearing rocks knew
of the men terrified
of a life loving
a man like me—
or do I mean that
the other way around?

• • •

I don't mean coffin, I don't mean
escape, more like
stars flamboyant in the black
mouth of night.

Revisions

Do not let him buy them, those pleated shorts, take off the cropped
black wig whose strands stuck to his face, let it be unknown how many
tapioca pearls he can eat in one sitting. Make us leave that grocery store,
never see the salted fish or strawberry flute straws. Please, unfall the
twenty-eight days of rain. Make us skip the workout of the day, unpush,
unpull. Unspeak the broken Vietnamese, silence the half conversations,
dial down the laughter. I've heard yesterday is just condensation on a
window, the day before an orb weaver's web. The streetlamp outside
my apartment started to flicker but now holds strong. It can be like that.
Let the tide recede, the bud unbloom. Make him step back through the
doorway, make him turn the lock back. Redact the news, those same four
headlines. At least redo the day of shopping, of him asleep on the drive
home. Do not let me break gently at any exit or stoplight, let me speed
and swerve. Let him startle and wake. Dear god, make him open his eyes.

Regrets, in the Style of Clue

Your ex at Home Depot with the mower
    blades and your cutoff jeans, or a mom
        in the dark garage, her face blossomed

plum, or a teen at clinic and his chipped
pink polish, or the sober juggalo
    at Red Cross with a matte black

        BB gun. The psychic by the door and spirits
    urging, *Trust him.* Your dead friend on the bridge
without wallet or phone, or yourself

    on the bridge with the bag
of chips. Your coach and the veins and callous
    grip and the *No man lifts*

because he's happy. Speech started
    and sputtered dead under the swing
        of a single bulb, or the drag queen

    denude of shadow and dress with the trust
fall to bed, or from his studio, the city
    behind the quilted curtains, or any black

        in your vision. Your friend in the cookie aisle
    and a tin of durian straws, with the ten-speed
in the quad and floodlights, with the snap-

    back in the gyms, with a keychain,
        with the triceps, with the dumplings,
    with the train set in the snowstorm,

with the statuesque man in the city,
    in the sun, in the closet, in a doorway,
        in a room that smells of laundry or copper.

Portraits of the Days' Griefs

Today's grief and I grope the man I've loved while the man he's loved
finds us coffee. Today's grief hurls the train not as late as forewarned, a
vanishing point reversed. Some days' griefs identify in third person femme
and they snap like a neon harness and sweat like virgin leather—you
can't throw these griefs in the wash. Last week's grief bleached me straw
and dander then tugged patch and bald. One morning's grief bled thin
down my windshield, the next day's slicked thick like jelly. I guess most
grief by grip and tread, but isn't all grief a failing brake? One day's grief
gifts a red jerk-off rash, the next wants to push its dick in dry, but honey
I begged spit on that kind of grief. In grief succession: seatmate quietly
sings opera through turbulent sky, two apples for dinner, pocketing a
pack of gum or a lady's purse or a jockstrap, I don't really care. One
night's grief split my lip and sucked the wound to clot. No grief has held
my body since, but still: a sting each time I kiss it goodnight.

Declaration with Immigrants' Child Eating Habits

I want you like durian
    like banned from the Marriot
        because other guests can
    smell our sweat
from their lonely beds
    Give me that soft pale center heavy
        spiked skin falling
    from branches like mango
with concussion Give me
    king prawn undressed
        before anyone wakes I want
    you like thick black coffee dripped
condensed milk
    I want you like evil
        chicken soup stoked
    hours until soft
like roast duck drumstick
    at a wedding—I will fight
        shirt sleeves rolled high
    for every last drop
of fat—I want
    a fried hog's head
        I want staring in my feast
    My fingers deep
in sacks of jasmine rice
    so tell me of handfeel
        of spilling into boil
    I want you plate
of oranges for the ancestors
    not mine yet but soon
        enough I want you firm
    gelatin flower I want you
scary to every mouth
    but mine I want you

microwave sign begging
No fish sauce
but I want it in public
loud and bold so walls
remember our scent

Treatise on Whether to Write the Mango

A missionary's pitch
was to ask if my grandma was planning
on Heaven and I was holding
     a box of mangos

when I couldn't think
of a response more than *yes* and slamming
the door with my right
     hip because a box of mangos

can jump from your arms so
eagerly, like during a fight with my mom
at the store that smelled like fish
     and she said *forget them*, the mangos,

because now they're sullied by ever-wet
foot paths and your ever-shitty teenage
attitude (*American!*), never clearer
     when I woke wanting mangos

instead of the rubbery jackfruit
she woke at dawn to peel
away from the thin white casing and so
     of course mangos

she had waiting, chilled
in the fridge after I missed family
dinner, sliced tic-tac-toe because
     only mango

flesh can yield so readily
to a blade or my grandma's
gums, teeth lost to the war,
     her skin hued and mangoed

with lack, with utter wanting
for home and the fist-sized
        yellow mangos,

though I (*American!*) prefer
the red-green ones the weight
of an unwell heart which is not
        the metaphor for mangos

you wanted right, you're used to small,
gentle breasts, juicy for your mouths
or some shit, but
        advice about mango

consumption: they're plucked
raw, inedible, and turn against you
while you sleep,
        to mush and mangle.

I Wrote a Poem with Faggot

for the first time. Flying my flaggot out
high, how it ribbons in the wind—god

what flamboyant youth, what emotional
baggot prevented this celebraggot

and naked joy. Scraggot loud with fierce
intention: I am Eric Traggot, I read

Kramer's cynical *Faggots* and was hard
as a raggot, angry, spilled teenage

saggot on those paggots of men fucking
into ruin and traggot. And still I pray

on my knaggot, shameless worship
of daggots, even boys who thraggoted

me with rocks were baggot, denial won't
staggot danger. Always on my lips, faggot

and smile, teeth and faggot, O faggot
faggot faggot faggot.

I Learned D&D When 45 Was Elected

I was a dwarven cleric, thick
book of devotions closing
wounds on the battlefield. I was
universal healthcare paid by thoughts
and prayers towards the long arc
of justice. I was a peasant
son who breathed best
in armor; I never showered
by choice but oiled my hinges
daily. I was leader during danger, so I led
us to danger. I was the bane
of snake-faced men, I shouted down
the sirens' false claims, I stole
from the fat dragon's
hoard. I was brought to death's
open bed and jumped in
myself. Most days I was
relentless with mercy. I never meant
to save, only to fight beside. I was mistaken
when I said thoughts and prayers. I meant
screaming a call to war.

Starting with a Line from a Minor Character in *Fury Road*

If you can't stand, you can't war. You can't water, you can't wicker, can't sunlight with coffee. You can't glory, can't trophy, can't chrome a week of plaque. Can't volume, can't bills, can't boxer briefs by the bed. Can't Kleenex, can't hard-on, can't dumpster to the curb. Can't skillet, can't flicker, can't goddamn can opener. Can't slipper, can't string of words, can't only fucking thing to make you smile lately. Can't sorry. Can't stand, can't gentle. Can't wait for gentle. Wake up, child. Sweetheart. Wake up, wake up, wake

Lectio Divina: Vision

The Vision #1

To his wife, who is also a synthezoid:
"The pursuit of an unobtainable purpose
by absurd means is the way of freedom;

                            this is my vision of the future.
                            Of our future. Do you see?"

. . .

A bowl is defined
by what it is not, my love,
hollowed by its calling.

                    What hell to be so full.
                    Let us be whole again;
                    let us empty it out.

. . .

I eased the needle into your creation,
filled quarts with his liver waste
until his delirious smile flattened.

                    We stared at each other, confused
                    and sheepish and soft, like two
                    bedmates waking up sober.

. . .

A thunderclap announcing
itself, bellowing itself
tantrum-tired:

                    gorgeous ripping,
                    internal wrestling
                    and then relief.

Amadeus Cho, Totally Awesome Hulk

At first I read trailblazing Asian hunk
then maybe thick, amorous, hung
and *kapow!* the punchline

is in the fiction. Because we can't
be hung, as in my cousin was named
Hung, Vietnamese for manly, brave

and had it legally changed at thirteen,
I'm sure you know why. Imagine:
forced to forfeit what your mother gave you

because of every person who's made dumb
jokes about eggrolls, about eyes slanted
like the eaves of buildings

in the rain. I hope you've never felt that,
Ammy. I hope you're as terrifying, aggressive,
and haughty as I devour in print. Quaking

the world with your steps. I wish
us your thunderous, amazing haunches.
Come green man, cousin,

let us be two-faced, ambitious,
hungry. Tactless Asian:

Toothy, artful, heroic.
Toxic, angry, hellish.

How to Pray

take the Eucharist / the body / the pulse / in your hand a book / of
matches / in the other / plums and potpourri / incense / the moon /
cakes your grandma sliced into eighths / a knife / your palm / pressed to
the other / draw a cross / a card / sell your Sabbath / bargain a bull / ask
for anything / but this right now / count beads until the anger sleeps /
beside you / gild the edges / gloss and guess / gist and djinn / fast or
purge / your belongings / any tether to the sod your father laid down /
taste the body / the crumbs and wine / what is blood but leaves / turning
season / to let the sun pass through / what is injury but preparation / be
willing / be wild / blueberries in summer / be forgiveness / like a small
dark box / be prostrate / be praise / an overflowing fountain / be a whistling
worried kettle / beg *shepherd / savior / take me off the fire / empty me out*

Hermione Granger and the Reciprocal Erasure

I _____ a memory _____

silent as ___ _____

_____ rainfall. ___ ____ ___ to remove

an oak tree is ___ __ ____ __ ____

but to never know it rooted.

So much __ _____ _____,

_____ as dreamless sleep

_____ ___ ____ _____ empty

buses commuting by _____

____ ___ _____ ____ rest

_____ _ ____ before pushing

forward again. Every breath

a chance __ _____.

. . .

_cast a _____ charm

_____ like the world

_____ _____. The best way __ _____

__ ___ ____ __ not to fell it down

___ __ ____ ___ __ _____.

__ ____ is unsayable already,

erased __ _ _____ _____

where you never heard _____

_____ _____ __ night.

Even the heart will try ____

after a beat _____ _____

_____ _____. _____ _____

__ _ _____ to forget.

Lectio Divina: Big Barda and Mister Miracle

Mister Miracle #5

Days after he cut open
his wrists, he says "You could
ask me, y'know. To stay.
I'd fight." And she says

"I can't . . . Scott, I told you. I'm not
your way out. All I can be
is your wife."

   • • •

In the dark, my love, I could be
your window of flame—but
to save the candle, you have to
snuff it out.

   • • •

I could have never let him
leave like the last webs of night.
I could have stood like a dune
against the tide.

   • • •

The sun lost ice to its own
embrace, to the roots
of maples whose leaves make
stars of their absence.

Closure

Soon you'll set down the grief
like a parent does an infant. It learns

to trail behind as an airless kite, mud prints
across the carpet, then a receipt

in your coat pocket whose ink you've thumbed
straight to ash. A hair in the soup

at a dinner party. You've learned to eat
around the intrusion or swallow it

politely and pray it passes through you,
not a line of stitches but the dimple

tucked under your sleeve, the song and thud
of an overhead fan, and apology

to the one-night stand, oh it's unbearable
to sleep without it.

Eclipse, One Month Before

It's too easy a metaphor, the sun not set

but stolen. The sudden cold and no place

to hide from penumbra. A wick gone

wet, gone winter, gone gray, and gone.

But here we are: betrayal, this brief cicada

-less summer. Or here I am, a single lack

of shadow calling you with nothing

to say but *I'm scared*. Silence everywhere,

but for now, even your breath is relief.

If You Had Asked What a Poem Meant

we hip-socket
tight sacroiliac
tight we

sacred fat
water skins
we   nothing

but water
to waste I
spill   take

sloped · hour
glass you
gnash chipped

porcelain tooth
you tongue
I silver

coin under
you silt bed

I slither
under you
I sliver

you fever
dream shards
I miss

all blood
vessels you
vena cava

returning dark
breathless   I miss
you calling

home I miss
you
          I miss you

Lectio Divina: *Black Bolt #6*

He has shattered
mountains with a word.
He has heard men say
that his shout can crack
a planet, and it might be true.

. . .

Break the book's spine
like a tangerine—thumbs
first, a quiet, lasting
hiss, then all that
sweet and sting.

. . .

I looked to poetry for grief.
See how words will collapse
into meaning? I sobbed
for your creation and his absence
followed into every line after.

. . .

The ground I believe
with both arched feet
heaving and crumbling
and look what's left:
a heap of memory,
crypt, volcano.

Portrait as Captain America Holding
a Helicopter with a Bicep Curl

Chris Evans thinks the scene
stupid, justice portrayed by a vanity

muscle. On green screen he struggled
against a crane and tore

a muscle because art requires
breaking your body a little, though I don't

stand behind that statement.
I've never loved one of my poems

as much as I love the feeling of one
I haven't written: insistent, radiant edges

in the dark I've made thick
for sleep, or a siren's song, the clanging

boomerang appeal pulling me
adrift the lane divide to dance

with another driver: what's a break
in the skin for one on the page?

I regret
that result already but, god, to be so

beautiful in the attempt, the glory
of pulling some brilliance closer.

When All That's Left Is Metaphor

Sum sinew of me aches
coal and ember. By night

dew I'm dying a hissing
heat. Embrace

me closing curtains
in wealth of nocturne.

Hold this head, river
and basket brimmed

with autumn leaves. Heavy
words, throwing stones

down a sinkhole. Or rest
them there. I've ignored

a friend's collapsing
cave to save my own

lonesome bed. I still want
quiet. Romance

this color: evening primrose;
this bloom for our gaze alone.

Aubade after Chemo

round one. Stubborn
pull-ups in the dark

before work. Slow,
weight-bearing, guilt

I can't share
the poison

in your blood. Limits
of two bodies, fire

of your veins
kept from mine

by skin. Give me new
words for aubade

because I don't sleep
anymore. When you leave

before dawn, I'm blind
but I follow a path

mapped by heat.

Untitled (Portrait of Ross in L.A.):
Mixed Material: Felix Gonzalez-Torres: 1991

Candies individually wrapped in multicolor cellophane, endless supply.
Dimensions vary with installation; ideal weight 175 lbs.

Certain by tins

　　　　　　of keratin Calcium　　　　strung flat

　　　　by candy floss

　　　　　　　　　　Pulsing　　　　homes traced

in gossamer Wrinkled

　　　　　　cellophane September

　　　　　　　　　　　　frost Constant

　　　ledge and shimmer

　　　　　　　meaning lost　　　　soon Faith hands

familiar　　　　to collapse

　　　　　　　　　　　Trigger　　　and thumb

open cotton skin

　　　　　　　　sighs swelled　　　　cracked

chapped Cheap　　　seams Still hands

　　　　　　　　　prints smear

on bathroom mirrors

claws   through honeycomb

Take sweetness   once and more

With teeth

In woolen palm

Other hand   barring gust

from soft and beating

straw and kindling

Self-Portrait as the Fire

-shredding axe-player

    in *Fury Road*. Blind

   adulation, licker thrust

peat-ward, lapping

    smogstack from

      your sweat glands.

 O burn my palate

worthy, char it

    black and bardic.

      Mute, I screech

   strings of fume

dreams: your desert breath,

   my soundless lips

    fellating sand.

I blast plumes

    of orange praise, scorched

   sky means I witness

by sonic heat, I witness

    sightless but sated,

        I witness my dermis

      singing into smoke.

Alternatives to Saying It

Sounds like bay door yawning open, bottle cap popped with iron rail.
Sorry, sounds not like *cancer*. Nothing like *sorry*. Like hard-packed
rubber, like bounce off plywood base. Knurled steel spinning—oh
whistle and catch, gasp and glottal stop. Catgut kissed felted air, fat
smoked across coal. River dive: crack like virgin femur, like unleavened
bread. Mower blade spinning rocks, mouthful of fork and china. OK so
velvet brushed napped and flat, but too no Velcro pulling free, no hooks
from lines of eye. Three phone rings and answer or shrill to voicemail.
Streetlight flicker: off and on, off and on, off and

Dear _____,

Here's how I fold fresh boxers
into short wings into the duffel

that sleeps under the bed
when not in the practice of leaving

the tiny pink house
I've always meant to paint

for you in a letter
but here's how a promise

undressed is just fortune-
telling is an evil eye

against a drought of tomorrows
and I could cast some bones

in the heart of your face
but really those first months without

every window cradled your face
until I learned to hold the grief

like an attic of heirlooms
and a single bulb

naked and waiting to be lit

Portrait as Orpheus, Ten Years Old

Already growing blind
     I lose my glasses again
walking Alex home,

      slipped from my backpack
somewhere past the practiced
      turn to my house, my mother

scared I've turned lost
      or worse. Even then I know
my decision is *bad*

      but I pretend not to see
every stepfall that could lead
      me backwards,

      only the dust of desert
lawns we kick back to life
      or the petal of light

I try to catch
      between the faces
of our shadows

Abstract

Objective   Two mouths

Materials   of feathers

Methods   colliding

Results   each kiss

Conclusions   a trial

                   of flight

Answers

for Daniel

You never asked, but it's overcast, the shade of both dawn and dusk
so the sun is both rising and setting. It's Schrödinger's cat on the
horizon. It's burnt rice in the pot, the loose hang of a tank top's neck.
It's discovering a dog-ear in a library book, it's knowing the most
important lines of your life before you've even met them.

It's riding your bike downhill, ass out of the seat, not worried about
traffic, the wind whistling in your ear's pinna—pure and solid. It's the
sound of a pile of quarters in your pocket that your grandma gave you
to get whatever you wanted at the 7-11, hell it's any kind of money
when the aunts get laid off again.

It's standing in line at the Griffith Observatory, the most visited
telescope stateside, it's a handful of tourists away from seeing Jupiter,
tolerating the guide who makes the same joke about each person
holding the new record, it's the little kid hogging the eyepiece because
he buys into it—for every second he stretches out, he's the most special
person in the world.

It's mango sliced around the pit, it's the rinds with teeth marks. It's a
worn-down callous, a string of green balloons. It's someone covering
your eyes—*Guess who*, they say, but what they're trying to ask is, *Who
else could it be?*

He Who Helps Drag Queens Descend the Stairs

You in the Abercrombie half-zip
made for someone who knows a decade less

of kindness. You who doesn't smile at dick jokes
or a queen tonguing her cheek to phantom

a blowjob, but who still offers dollars bookmarked
between fingers or resting in your palm

opened like a leaf. Who taught you this devotion,
the unassuming necessity of a single spotlight,

of the glue behind the glitter, the links above
the chandelier? You patron/saint of

the naked, unrolled ankle
strapped in a high heel. You harbinger

of a spandex pantheon, you gel-tipped
trumpeter. Here, background music

is *heralding*. Take up your brassy horn,
press it to your lips and blow.

Garden

Then let's plant a garden
with the memories that keep
me awake. They'll grow

together, you and what
I didn't tell you
about my backyard,

like Sundays saved
for weeding the wings
of dill, first clumsy

handfuls through work
gloves then held like
quills between my farthest

fingers. I am allergic
to everything green and still,
I keep flowers in vases

outside my door, even
the bouquet you worried
never made it

to me, days anxious
if a neighbor got my roses.
Maybe I wrote this poem

to say I'm sorry
if loving me was stressful
or when I tell people

I love them now
your name's the antecedent
so every bud or reliable

fig tree I prune before
the hurricane is proof
you're still alive

to me. Or I'm sorry,
I blur the borders
between tribute and denial.

Or love isn't just stress
all the time. Here:
a corner of the garden,

where at ten I planted
corn—corn!—in our desert
soil, yards from any sprinkler

but still it grew, without fear
of joy or shame and faster
than I could eat

but mostly it was thing
to witness, to marvel, so much
growing out of almost nothing.

NOTES AND ACKNOWLEDGMENTS

Lectio divina, divine reading, is a monastic practice of approaching a sacred text. I owe a debt to the podcast *Harry Potter and the Sacred Text* for introducing this to me.

New X-Men #122 was written by Grant Morrison

Saga #9 was written by Brian K. Vaughan

Mister Miracle #5 was written by Tom King

The Vision #1 was written by Tom King

Thank you to the editors of the following journals for publishing these poems, sometimes in different forms.

Figure 1: "Regrets, in the Style of Clue"
Four Way Review: "Pulse" and "He Who Helps Drag Queens Descend the Stairs"
IDK Magazine: "Starting with a Line by Joyce Byers"
Juked: "Explaining Again Why I Can't Give Blood" and "Portrait in Pleather Tee"
Lambda Literary Poetry Spotlight: "I Wrote a Poem with Faggot"
New Delta Review: "Eloisa—"
North Carolina Literary Review: "Treatise on Whether to Write the Mango"
Prairie Schooner: "I Tell My Mother about My Depression," "Ode to My Morning
    Meds," and "Lectio Divina: Big Barda and Mister Miracle"
The Shallow Ends: "Portraits of the Days' Griefs"
Slice Literary Magazine: "Amadeus Cho, Totally Awesome Hulk"
Sou'wester: "Lectio Divina: Emma Frost" and "Days after Orlando I Read the
    X-Men"
Superstition Review: "Alternatives to Saying It"
Tinderbox Poetry Journal: "Answers"
Voicemail Poems: "My Mother Asks How I Was Gay before Sleeping with a Man"
wildness: "Compromise"

"Eloisa—" won the 2015 Matt Clark Editor's Prize as "Bathhouse Haibun."

"My Mother Asks Me How I Was Gay before Sleeping with a Man" was featured in *Best of the Net 2015*.

"Treatise on Whether to Write the Mango" was a finalist for the 2019 James Applewhite Poetry Prize.

Some of these poems appeared in *Revisions*, a chapbook published by Sibling Rivalry Press.

I am deeply grateful for the presence and generosity of:

The editors and staff at Autumn House Press and Stacey Waite for believing in this book. And Bryan Borland and Seth Pennington at Sibling Rivalry Press for their fierce support of my work.

The Travelers' Club: Regina DiPerna, Nathan Johnson, Whitney Ray, Anna Sutton, and Gabriella R. Tallmadge. You have made me and my poetry braver and richer. I love you all.

My mentors and teachers: Jo Ann Beard, Bekki Lee, Sarah Messer, Ocean Vuong. And the professors and staff (especially Robyn Latessa, Kathy Meachem, Ira Sloan) at the University of North Carolina School of Medicine, Asheville Campus for allowing me the space to write. And my classmates: Ray Antonelli, Rob Broadhurst, Amelia Cline, Ben Frush, Daniel Gardner, Sarah Lowder, Nathan Markiewitz, Franklin Niblock, and Mona Xiao, for reminding me poetry was still important.

My biological and chosen families: my parents, my grandmother, my aunts and uncle, Jonathan Nguyen, Joyce Dela Pena, Erik Donhowe, Devin Lee, Jamie Tam. I would be nowhere without you.

And Zach Doss, for showing me how beautiful and joyous life could be.

ERIC TRAN is a resident physician in psychiatry at the Mountain Area
Health Education Center, with particular interest in LGBT mental health
and addiction medicine. He graduated from the University of North
Carolina Chapel Hill's School of Medicine, where he received the Alan C.
Cross Award and the Heusner Pupil Award. He also holds an MPH from
the University of North Carolina at Chapel Hill and received his MFA
from the University North Carolina Wilmington. He is the author of the
chapbooks *Revisions* (Sibling Rivalry Press, 2018) and *Affairs with Men
in Suits* (Backbone Press, 2014). His work appears in such publications
as *Missouri Review, 32 Poems, Indiana Review, Pleiades* and has received
awards and recognition from *Best of the Net, New Delta Review, North
Carolina Literary Review,* and others. He is from the San Francisco Bay
Area and currently lives in Asheville, North Carolina with his many plants
and shoes.

New and Forthcoming Releases

For our full catalog please visit: http://www.autumnhouse.org